J. DOUGLAS BARRY

MEMOIRS OF AN ABUSED CHILD

Copyright @2020 by J. Douglas Barry

All rights reserved. No part of this book may be reproduced in any form or by any electronic or mechanical means, including information storage and retrieval systems, without permission in writing from the publisher, except by reviewers, who may quote brief passages in a review.

This publication contains the opinions and ideas of its author. It is intended to provide helpful and informative material on the subjects addressed in the publication. The author and publisher specifically disclaim all responsibility for any liability, loss or risk, personal or otherwise, which is incurred as a consequence, directly or indirectly, of the use and application of any of the contents of this book.

WORKBOOK PRESS LLC
187 E Warm Springs Rd,
Suite B285, Las Vegas, NV 89119, USA

Website: https://workbookpress.com/
Hotline: 1-888-818-4856
Email: admin@workbookpress.com

Ordering Information:
Quantity sales. Special discounts are available on quantity purchases by corporations, associations, and others.
For details, contact the publisher at the address above.

ISBN-13:   978-1-953839-09-1 (Paperback Version)
           978-1-953839-10-7 (Digital Version)

REV. DATE: 04/11/2020

PART I: STORY OF AN ABUSED CHILD

I dedicate this work to two African American children living in Tallahassee, Florida.

They were both born in the 1960's and grew up dirt poor. I haven't seen either of them since August 1979 when I left Tallahassee to move to Hingham, Massachusetts to enter the Maryknoll Seminary. Whether they are both still alive, and are both still dirt poor, as I imagine they are, I don't know.

To Annette and Ida Francis Corbett, my dear friends, I dedicate this work.

January 9, 2017

I

It was a cold winter day in Scarsdale, New York 1948. For a four-year-old boy, there seemed to be snow everywhere. Even after sixty-eight years, I remember what I was wearing, perhaps because of what was about to happen on this bright, sunny day.

I was with my neighborhood friends, and I was wearing a grey jacket, a hat, gloves and black boots with silver buckles. My friends and I were playing outside an open garage at the house that was behind mine, back and up to the left. I recall an African American lady dressed in white at the back of the garage calling me to come in. I did as she asked and within a foot or two of the garage, I looked down at the boots and they were both smoking. The next thing I remember was that the skin on the middle of my right leg was beginning to burn and I was feeling intense pain.

I leapt for the outside of the garage and began rolling around in the snow. My screams alerted my nanny, Eva, as I recall seeing her running across our back yard. That was the last thing I remember.

Later, I was told my father, a senior partner with a Wall Street investment firm, was called and flew up in a helicopter to the Westchester airport. I don't remember any time in the hospital. I do, however, recall my sister, Carol, and I spending time in Bermuda for my recuperation. There was a picture taken of us at the ocean's edge showing the severe burn on my right leg. Years later, when my mother took me to a doctor, she introduced him as the doctor "who saved my leg".

My father sued the family who owned the house where I was burned for $600, with $200 going to the lawyer and the remaining $400 to me.

I never did tell my family about the maid who called me into the garage in the first place. As I look back on it, I am sure the good Lord was protecting me from whatever she had in mind.

II

Within a couple of years, when I was six, my father bought a large colonial house, also in Scarsdale. There were four floors with six white columns at the front. All the bedrooms were on the third floor, except one which was just off the kitchen. It was this bedroom where my nanny, Eva, lived.

Two stairwells went up to the third floor, one in the back which I don't remember that well, and one off the front entry hall. This was a winding staircase, with green carpet and white bannister. Every Christmas season, the bannister was decorated in a garland of green holly and Christmas balls, making it an extremely festive season.

I recall in 1950 when I was six years old and we were newly moved into the house, I wanted to take a freshly squeezed glass of orange juice up to my big brother Gene. Gene was ten years older and played football at Scarsdale High School, the same school I would attend in nine years.

I don't remember what month it was, nor what season, but I do recall my Aunt "Lady" was visiting.

I carefully carried the juice up the many stairs to my brother's bedroom at the top of the stairs. I ever so quietly opened the door. (As far as I knew, six-year-old boys didn't knock on doors.). As I opened the door, I noticed my brother was sleeping. So, as quietly as I could, I placed the glass of juice on his night table and just as quietly turned to leave and closed the door behind me, not knowing that this last action
must have been what woke him up.

It's hard to remember everything that happened on this fateful day, sixty-six years ago, but I believe I had a contented smile as I carefully went down the stairs.

As I reached the bottom of the stairs, my brother came out of his room in a rage. He had one of his football shoes in his hand, the kind with metal cleats. He hurled the shoe at my head and his accuracy was right on, with the cleats landing square on top of my head.

I, of course, let out a blood curdling yell. The blood so covered my face that when my mother and aunt came out of the kitchen where they were preparing breakfast, they could not tell which child it was because of the blood.

After this, the only thing I remember is my brother yelling from inside his bedroom "He woke me up!" To the best of my recollection, it was the only time my mother ever took a belt to one of her five children. But I bet he drank that orange juice and enjoyed it.

My brother, however, was not done with his abusing either me or my family. A few years later, while I was in the den watching TV and lying on the floor, I heard from upstairs my oldest sister yell "He hit me!" This incident might have been the first, but certainly not the last. After my father died, at 52 and I was eleven, my mother wrote two letters, one to my brother and one to my oldest sister. The letters were almost identical, asking them to take the initiative. It was up to them to meet their sibling halfway, that our family could not go on with this constant fighting. She told them she was confident that their sibling would treat them with love and respect if they would make the first move to be conciliatory. It worked. The arguing stopped. My mother
told me to never tell either of them about the letters. She wanted each one to believe they had received the only letter.

Very many years later, after having served in the Marine Corps and subsequently graduating from college, I came home, to my mother's New York apartment. Right after graduation, I obtained an overnight ride with three other recent graduates. When we arrived in New York City, I invited my new friends up to meet my mother and have some sandwiches made for their continued journey. My brother was in "his chair" in the living room watching TV. I don't know what prompted him, but he said, "I am so glad I never went to college." I suppose he was under the false impression I would come home, having majored in philosophy, with words of wisdom 24/7. Needless to say, it doesn't work that way.

After all this, there was still one more person for him to abuse: my mother.

This was another time when I, my brother and my mother were still living in Manhattan. It was a rainy morning and my mother was still asleep. I was within earshot of my mother's bedroom when my brother opened his bedroom door and went to the edge of mother's room. He clearly saw she was sound asleep, but this to my brother was no hindrance to what he desired. "Mom?" No response. "Mom?" Still no response and he persisted until she awoke. "Gene, what is it?" Whenever any of her five children needed something, she always responded immediately.

"Can you get my breakfast?"

"Gene, I was asleep."

"Oh, you were?", as if he didn't know. But my ever kind mother responded. "What do you want?"

"Well, it's a French toasty day," his reaction whenever it rained or snowed, or even when it was overcast and gloomy. "So, how about French toast and bacon?" Mother knew the unspoken words were orange juice and fresh coffee. (He never drank instant coffee when my mother was the cook.)

"All right. Just give me time to get dressed."

My brother never physically abused my mother, only me and my sister. Call it what you may, but his treatment of my mother was abuse. I'm sure he never looked at it that way, just so long as his needs were being met.

Then, on the day of my mother's funeral, upon leaving the cemetery where my father and grandparents are buried, he had the gall to cry on my oldest sister's shoulder. Of course, my sister was as compassionate and loving as my mother and comforted him in our loss. It was more than he deserved.

III

Going back to the continued abuse of my childhood, in the summer of 1952, my parents sent me to a camp in the Adirondacks, with my three sisters at a girls' camp nearby. Right away, I did not like the camp, as they had us go outside in our pajamas to pledge allegiance to the flag, regardless of the cold and rainy weather.

I remember very little of the camp except, of course, the abuse.

These things children never seem to forget.

In 1952, I was eight years old. I recall I was in my bathing suit and standing in front of the lake. I was hesitant to go in, first because I hadn't been taught to swim and second, there were a lot of rocks. The counselor told me to jump in. I told him there were rocks there, but he persisted. So, as a trusting eight-year-old, raised to listen to and obey adults, I jumped in! The result is I got cut up and bruised by the rocks. When I came up out of the lake, I wasn't crying, but I was bleeding. The counselor told me to go to the camp nurse. When I told her, what happened and why I had jumped in, she could not believe it. Back in the 1950's, people tended not to believe a child when the child spoke of abuse by an adult, whether it be physical, mental or sexual.

When my oldest sister came to visit me at camp, she saw right away the obvious abuse I had undergone. She immediately called my father and he flew up and mercifully took me out of that camp.

A year later, in 1953, when I was nine, my parents sent me to a camp in Vermont. I went there for nine years and was the only Catholic boy in my cabin. There were a few Catholics at the camp and we were driven to Mass each Sunday. One Sunday after Mass, I returned to my cabin to change into shorts and t-shirt to join the other campers. When I left the cabin, everything was in proper order, beds made, trunks closed. But when we came back about an hour later, everything was awry. All the beds and trunks had been overturned, except mine! This caused suspicion of me and no one believed that I had been set up. In fact, the way they all acted, I don't even think they ever considered that possibility. They repeatedly questioned me and did not believe me when I said I did not do it.

Eventually, the last person to question me was the Head Counselor, who told me I could not go to lunch unless I confessed. I started crying, at which point he stopped his questioning and accusations. I
was allowed to go to lunch and nothing more was said that summer. Nothing, that is, until the following year, 1954. That summer, after Mass, I again returned to a well-kept cabin to change clothes. And once again when we returned the cabin was in disarray. All the beds and trunks had been overturned, except mine. The axe really came down on me. The Head Counselor was relentless. I told the truth again. Did they really think I'd be so stupid as to upset everyone's belongings except my own?

The real culprit was never discovered. Perhaps it was someone who hated Catholics. I was the only one in my cabin in 1953 and 1954.

As disconcerting as this was, the worst of the abuse was yet to come, and this time, it was physical abuse.

In 1954, I had two camp counselors that were about 18 years old. One night, they woke me up and told me to go to the next cabin and tell the counselor, Bill Brown, some nonsensical thing. He was sound asleep, so I woke him up to do as I was told. He was a light sleeper and fortunately for me loved children. He told me to return to my cabin and when I got into my bunk bed, I realized my sheets were soaking wet. The counselors accused me of being a bed-wetter. I told them I had been the previous year, but no longer was. They said they'd change the sheets and sent me back to Bill Brown in the next cabin with another nonsensical story. I did as they asked and when I returned to my cabin, they had put three broomsticks under the covers of my bed. By this time, the other campers were awake and laughing. When I got out of bed this time, one of the counselors struck me. I was not going to take this abuse anymore. I grabbed one of the brooms and started to fight back. One counselor knocked the broom out of my hands and held my arms back while the other slapped me in the face and punched me. With all the noise I was making and the yells of the other campers, the counselor, Bill Brown, in the next cabin came down and grabbed both counselors and took them to the camp director. I never saw them again. I never told my parents about this incident. I came back to the camp for seven more years, ultimately becoming a counselor myself.

IV

On January 21, 1956, my father passed away at the young age of 52. I was eleven. Shortly after this, a neighbor began to sexually abuse me. He told me what to do and being a child, I did it. I don't remember how many times this happened, at least three times, maybe more. After being raped, I began to stutter. No one knew why I was stuttering. I didn't know why.

I was in elementary school at the time. There was a very nice young woman who was a student assistant teacher. As I had a learning disability, she was working with me. She knew something was bothering me and asked me what was wrong. I never told her. I kind of wish she had persisted. The sexual abuse happened a few more times and the stuttering continued for many more years. Perhaps if she had discovered the problem, it would have stopped. But back then, who had ever heard of a child being sexually abused? If they had, it was not something people talked about.

My stuttering got so bad that there were times when I was confronted about it, I reached the point where every word was difficult to pronounce, even my own name. Then, in 1965, I dropped out of college to enter the Marine Corps. The first time I stuttered in front of my Junior Drill Instructor (DI), Sgt. Perdue, he slapped me full force in the face. He said he would slap me every time I stuttered. This had a temporary effect of stopping my stuttering, but as soon as I was honorably discharged from the Marine Corps, my stuttering returned. Not until I was a student at Florida State University was, I completely cured of what to me was a disease. In fact, I can thank Dr. Tom Allan who told me something that cured me.

V

That slap that Sgt. Perdue gave me was just the beginning of the abuse I experienced at the hands of my three DIs, Sgts. Pope, Purdue and Paro. They not only beat me and the other ninety recruits, but they tortured, humiliated and generally mistreated young men who were prepared to give their lives for their country, and most of them did in the Vietnam War, a war that took over 57,000 American lives.

I remember the first night in Parris Island, there was a lot of yelling going on. The recruit next to me was shaking all over. I told him that this was just yelling, that they were not going to beat us. Boy, was I wrong? The very next day, the beatings began, and he was the first one they got rid of.

I don't recall the order in which the beatings came, but I remember each one. For example, I remember we had returned to the Squad Bay and my upper bunk mattress had been overturned on the floor. Sgt. Perdue came down the center of the Squad Bay and asked whose bunk that was. I called out "Private Barry, Sir". He then said, "Why wasn't that bed tight?" I said, "I thought it was sir." That was the wrong thing to say, as he punched me as hard as he could in the gut.

Then there was the time when we had been there about a week, and the training was the toughest thing I had ever been through. I sought out my three DIs to tell them I didn't believe I could do it. That night, my Senior DI, Sgt. Pope, took me into his room, closed the door and told me to get on my knees. He then took a bottle of Tabasco sauce and holding the bottle in front of his groin, started pouring the hot sauce into my open mouth. When he felt he had poured enough, he asked me a question. Once I answered, the pain in my throat was intolerable. The following day at what was called "School Circle", he asked me in front of the rest of the platoon if I still wanted to quit. I jumped up and said, "No Sir!".

The very first night I learned something about our meals. Some of the recruits began having cups of milk passed to their seats from the recruit sitting next to the milk dispensary. I began thinking of asking for the same pleasure when the DI put an immediate stop to that. In fact, that was the last meal that any of us was allowed any liquid of any kind.

There was one exception. I was on the rifle range and in addition to the beating I got for not qualifying on the first day, to the crawling on my stomach from my Squad Bay to the next saying "unq, unq, unq", I also wasn't allowed the customary three meals for two days, but I was allowed a cup of milk in its stead.

Milk was not the only beverage we were not allowed. For the eight weeks we were there, we were not allowed any water, even after a three-mile run on a hot day. They even watched us in the showers and told us not to drink the water. My thirst got so bad I came very close to drinking the dirty water I had just mopped the floor with because no one was watching. Why there was a water fountain there, or why we had canteens on our belts when we were told to get our "war gear" on is beyond my understanding.

One last thing to tell about the treatment at the barracks occurred at the rifle range: I don't know if this was standard treatment for all recruits, or just for my platoon. All ninety of us were given wooden clothespins and told to wear them on our trigger finger all the time we were standing in the Squad Bay, which was a lot of the time. I was experiencing a great deal of pain on my index finger of my right hand. When I felt I could get away with it, I did whatever I could to relieve the pressure on my finger.

The reason for using the clothespin, according to Sgt. Pope was to make our trigger finger so sore we would be barely able to squeeze the trigger of our M-14, that it would increase the accuracy of our firing.

Although after 52 years, I am sure I don't remember all the beatings, for they seemed to be constant, there are still some that stand out. Like the recruit who was in the bunk next to me. The lights were out and he began whispering my name looking for a response. I knew enough to ignore him and did not answer. He called my name a second time, not knowing that our Senior DI was quietly patrolling the Squad Bay. In a silent and deliberate action, the DI came down on the private's arm, breaking it in half. He then placed his hand over his mouth and told him to go to the medical center in the morning and tell the corpsman he slipped in the shower room. I remember this so well not because it happened to me, but because I listened to the private crying in pain all night. To this same private there was another incident of significance. He crapped in his pants, something a Marine never does. I won't even begin to tell you the terrible pain he experienced at the hands of the four squad leaders, who were under instructions from Sgt. Pope, our Senior DI.

There was the time we had been outside marching. The Junior DIs, Sgts. Perdue and Paro, told us to do something in the march and we did something else. That was it. They immediately marched us back to the Squad Bay and started asking for gloves. They didn't want to injure their hands, nor did they want to leave any marks on our bodies. They then went down the line and beat all ninety of us one by one. There was a private posted at each of the two Squad Bay doors who were told to yell "Stand By" just as soon as anyone came.

As far as being reported, they told us that if we did tell, they would be told there was going to be an investigation and that before they were removed from the platoon, platoon 395, they would be left alone with us for 24 hours, and then they would beat us. After they were removed and the investigation began, our training would stop. We would be marched to and from chow three times a day and then just sit in the Squad Bay. The investigation could take up to a month. We would get lazy, put on weight and when new DI's came in, it would be like starting all over.

Sgt. Perdue told us another time that if anyone wanted to fight him, we would go into the head and fight, but win or lose, when it was over, we were going to the brig.

In the first week of being at Boot Camp, the DIs gave us a choice: If we screwed up, we could either do physical exercise or be punched as punishment, and then it would be over. We trusted them, wanting to become Marines ourselves, so we all agreed to the punching. At the time, a single punch seemed innocent enough. Problem was it was a lot more than that.

There were times when some of us were singled out for a beating, like the time it was getting cold and we were told we could wear insulated long sleeve shirts. It was cold enough for all ninety of us to wear them. We were marched to some activity where we had been told to take off the insulated shirts. Doing this showed that about ten of us, including me, did not have on t-shirts. When we got back to the Squad Bay, Sgt. Perdue called the ten of us into his room. He asked why we did not have on t-shirts. I was the first to respond and said, "I thought we had permission to wear the insulated shirt." He said, "You do, but not without a t-shirt, understand?" I said, "Yes Sir!" and he punched me in the gut, hard. He said, "You are not supposed to think."

Once, something occurred that even now does not make any sense. We were all marched over to another platoon behind some buildings. We were there to compete in a rope "tug-of-war". There was a large ditch between the two platoons. We took up the rope and began to pull. Sgt. Pope told us to stop pulling and just hold. This we did. He continued to encourage us to hold. As the other platoon began to struggle in their pulling, our DI yelled at us to pull. We did. By now, as we pulled with ease, we pulled the other platoon into the large ditch in the middle. However, the pride we felt at our success was immediately brought to an end. Our Senior DI told us to close ranks, put our heads down and push up against each other as close as we could. He then marched us back to the Squad Bay in shame that we had won the "tug-of-war". Like I said, this did not make any sense then and does not to this day.

Toward the end of Boot Camp, when I had become extremely strong, we were all doing bends and thrusts. It got to the point where the platoon was going up and I was going down. Then they were going down and I was going up. The Senior DI came over and stood right in front of me. He then told us to run in place. As we did, he punched me in the chest three times as hard as he could. I never even moved. He then stopped punching me.

Another time he slapped me occurred when my glasses broke and needed repair. I took them to Sgt. Pope. He rose from his chair and slapped me in the face with all his might. I had no idea why he did this and just stood there dumbfounded. He then explained why he slapped me. I don't recall what his lame excuse was.

VI

When I was discharged from the Marine Corps, I felt confident that I would encounter no more physical abuse and this was true. Yet there were other ways that people would eventually find, such as verbal abuse and intimidation, as I found when in January of 1985, I went to work for the Internal Revenue Service in Andover, Massachusetts.

I was employed as a tax examining assistant, first for the section that was handling individual tax returns and second in the section known as BMF Business Tax Returns. It was in this latter section that over a period of nine years, 1985-1993, that I encountered both the verbal abuse and the intimidation, leveled by one person, and one person only, my supervisor.

For example, we had sheets of paper, called "3081", on which we recorded the time we worked. One day, the lady supervisor walked in front of our unit of about 35 people. She had a single "3081" in her hand. She then asked, "Who turned in a '3081' without signing it?" No response. So, she called out again in a louder voice, intimidating the employees with her obese size of probably 300 pounds. "Who turned in a '3081' without signing it?" Still, no one answered. Her next statement I'm sure shocked some, surprised others and did not even phase the seasoned few who were used to her ways. She paused a few seconds and then in a loud voice said, "When I find out, I'm going to beat the shit out of you," with emphasis on the foul word.

For four years, while working for the IRS, I had been studying the martial arts after work at a school in Haverhill. In addition to this, I was running every day from one to three miles, first along Route 133 in Georgetown and then Route 28 in Andover. I was in excellent physical condition and had the physique to show it. One day at work, at the Andover Service Center, I needed some blank forms out of the large shelving where we kept all our forms. I needed to squat down to retrieve a form and shortly after squatting down, I overheard my supervisor say, "Doug has a nice butt." Sounds like sexual harassment to me, but why not. She got away with everything and she knew it.

After six or seven years, I was promoted to the Lead Tax Examining Assistant. In addition to all the tax forms that my supervisor set up for me to process, I had the duties of the Lead. This included teaching the other employees how to process business tax returns, reviewing their work and filling out employee quality reports, the latter being a requirement for which I had little time.

I mentioned this concern to my supervisor and her remark, without a moment's hesitation was "to lie" on the forms. And, at first, I did, but not for long because I had a conscience.

In the Federal Government, at least within the Internal Revenue Service, we have a department known as "Inspection". They are supposed to investigate any and all reported incidents of fraud or as I understood it, anything that was inappropriate. I went to this unit behind closed doors and spoke with the first man I came in contact with. I told him of the entire situation, believing that everything I said in this office was confidential. And maybe it was, but there was a young woman in that office making photocopies. Within a day or two, while I was sitting at my desk in the unit, a group of supervisors and the Section Chief came walking up to my supervisor. She looked at them coming towards her and asked, "Am I in some kind of trouble?"

I had no idea that they were telling her what I did. I then overheard one of the lady supervisors say, "I can't believe he did that!" Later, I realized that she was of course denying that she told me to lie and that I was a habitual liar.

Being aware of what had just happened, at my break, I called the investigator to whom I had spoken and asked him if he had told anyone of our conversation. He said he had not, so I told him I had noticed a young woman making photocopies right near his desk while I was speaking with him. Not only did he not respond, as I remember, but I never heard from him again.

A few weeks after this incident, while I was walking back to the unit with my supervisor, she again instructed me to lie about something, although I don't recall what it was.

Now that I have been diagnosed with osteoarthritis in my left hand and degenerative joint disease in my right, I am required to wear a brace on both hands to minimize the pain. As it is, every letter I print is met with some discomfort. Whenever I go down the stairs, if I haven't had a cortisone shot in both of my knees, the pain can be intense.

I mention this just to show the kind of person my supervisor was. Many years ago, back when I was still working at the IRS, I mentioned to someone in my unit that I had been diagnosed with severe arthritis, although I wasn't experiencing any pain associated with this condition at the time. For some reason, I turned my head to look back at my supervisor and here she was looking me right in the eye with a large grin on her face. I didn't see the humor in that then, and I sure don't now.

Every day, when we went to work at the IRS, we found wagons next to our desks that were completely filled with business tax forms which had to be processed. Each wagon was filled with eight hours of work with 1/2 hour allowed for lunch, as well as two fifteen-minute breaks. Our supervisor became really upset if the work was not completed in the allotted time.

One day, before I became the Lead, I arrived at my desk with two wagons filled with work to be processed. At the end of the day with both my speed and my accuracy, I was able to complete the processing of both wagons. Subsequently, I confided in my Lead that the work that had been set up for me was not eight hours but nine. I overheard the Lead tell the supervisor that my work was nine hours' worth, not the customary eight. Then I heard her answer, "I know. I just wanted to see if he could do it." So, I busted my butt to please what was a whim of my supervisor.

Time passed, days, weeks, even months, I don't remember. But the day came when I showed up at work to a full wagon of returns to be processed. At the end of the day, while I was pushing the wagon to the back of the unit, my supervisor asked me if I finished the wagon she set up. I calmly said "no". She then, at the top of her lungs yelled "Why?" I had gotten to the point where I was fed up with her yelling, her foul mouth, her attempts at intimidation and finally her trying to throw her oversize weight around. With all my might, I pushed the wagon I had up against the wall and the wagon toppled over. On the other side of the red brick wall was the office of the Branch Manager, Bob. I don't remember his last name. He immediately came out of his office to see the wagon lying on the floor. I then said "Sorry, Bob". I don't recall what he responded, but whatever he said, I did not respond.

I heard my supervisor say, "Tomorrow morning, I'm going to talk to him about what just happened." She then stood up and left her desk to go home. I don't know if the Branch Manager talked to her, or if during the night, she thought better about it, but neither the next morning, nor any time after that did, she talk to me about that incident.

VII

In conclusion, this life-long abuse, abuse by my neighbor at the age of four, the abuse at the two camps, the sexual abuse and especially the torture and inhumane treatment at the hands of the U. S. Marine Corps brought on a life-long effect, i.e., my living life as a weak man. Instead of coming out of the Marine Corps as fearless, I came out fearful, fearful of confronting people I didn't know and especially of being disagreeable with anyone for fear that they would yell at me.

Only recently have I changed and become strong. I am now ready to stand on my own two feet. Those who have known me all my life, I believe, are beginning to notice a difference, and if not, ask me if I care.

What you have just read is the absolute truth.

AUTHOR'S PRECIOUS GALLERY

Me outside my apartment in Andover, MA. My beard not that long now.

My mother Margaret. Now deceased.

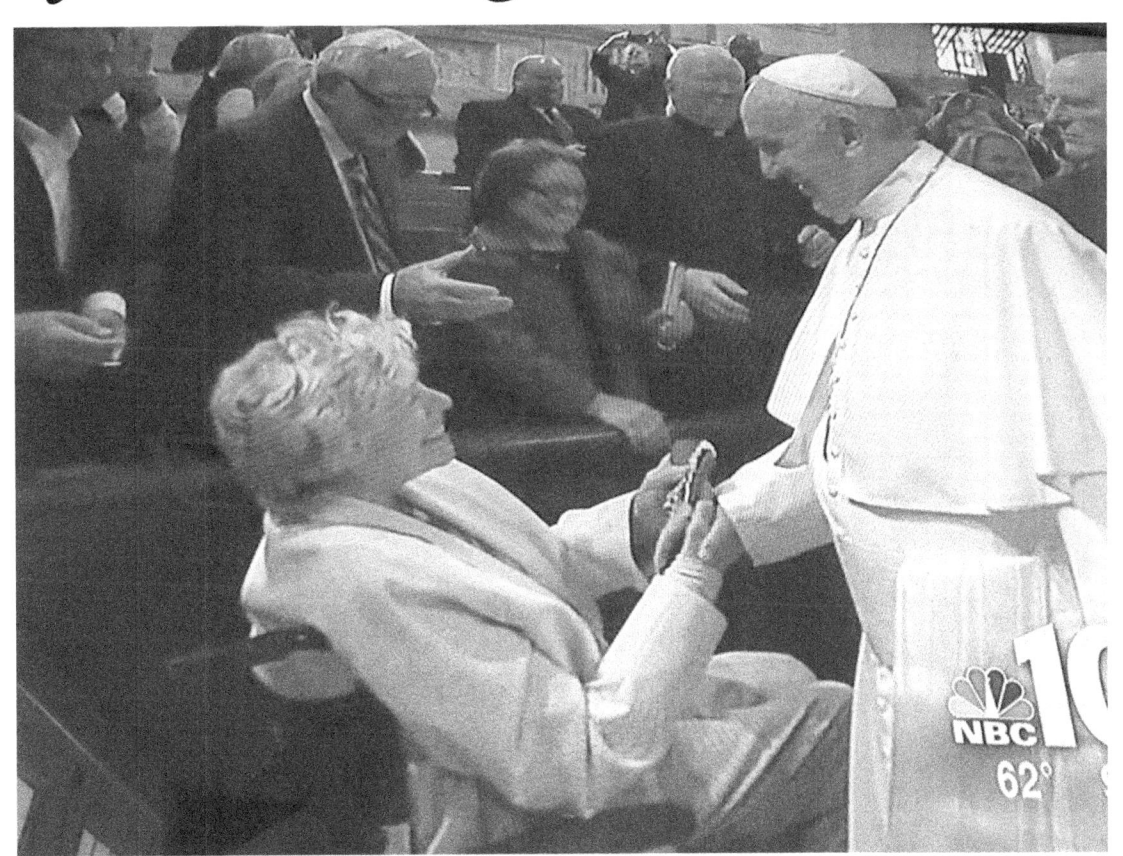

My sister Margo with Pope Francis in Philadelphia

My youngest sister Faith at my sister Margo's Shore house in Avalon, NJ

My middle sister Carol also at Margo's Shore house.

My father Eugene Barry who died at age fifty-two when I was only eleven.

Me cooking dinner at my sister Margo's home in Gladwyne, PA on Christmas Day.

My father again in front of the home I grew up in in Scarsdale, NY. With the Virgin Mary keeping him company.

My brother-in-law Dan Polett standing in front of the Scarsdale, NY home I grew up in.

Outside my apartment in winter in Andover, MA

Top pic of me and Faith at four and three. Bottom pic of me, Faith and Carol in the library of our Scarsdale home on Brewster Road.

Photo of my parents when first married

My library in my living room. About 100 history and religious books.

Me and my four siblings at my sister Margo's shore home in Avalon, NJ since that photo I've taken off eighty-two pounds.

My very best friend Ida Frances Corbett. Now deceased

Me after being awarded my First-Degree Green belt in Martial Arts.

Taken before I lost eighty pounds a few years ago.

Fall in New England

PART II: DEAR MARC

DEAR MARC

A Collection of Miracles

by

J. Douglas Barry

Dear Marc

So, you don't believe in the existence of God!

06-05-20

Let me tell you about my personal and TRUE life experiences and see what you believe then.

I am a 76-year-old retired U.S. Marine. I only mention this because Marines don't lie, or at least this Marine doesn't lie.

Back in 1968 when I was attending Florida State University in Tallahassee, I decided to walk the two miles to the movie theatre that was showing one of Clint Eastwood's "spaghetti westerns". I had no transportation other than my own two feet. When the movie ended, it was late and dark. As I made my way back to my off-campus apartment, I began wondering if I could find a shortcut. When I came to a residential street on my left, I decided to try it. There was a slight incline in the road and as I climbed it, I began to hear some dogs barking. I saw two small dogs running toward me. Feeling this was a bad idea, I turned around and began to make my way back to I-90, the highway I had just left.

By now, those two dogs had alerted the neighborhood. Shortly, I was completely surrounded by at least ten dogs of all kinds and sizes, with more running toward me.

My initial instinct was to defend myself by attack, so as I squatted down to a Martial Arts position, I growled. Well, at first, all the dogs jumped back, but this just angered them even more and they came closer attempting to bite my legs. I then squatted down as before and yelled as loud as I could and once more, this frightened them. Again, all ten dogs jumped back, but only for a moment. They were now overwhelmed with ferocious anger. This was a losing situation, so I did the only thing I knew to do. I said, "St. Jude, protect me." And with this, ALL of the dogs stopped barking, turned around and walked away. I, of course, immediately headed back to I-90 and went home.

This is the first of many such miracles that have happened to me.

Let me ask you, Marc. Why do you think I have become friends with your brother, Benoit? I would say because God knows you and loves you. Just remember this: eternity is a very long time.

Still don't believe in God. One more miracle.

I am diabetic. I have been since February 2006. Two weeks after diagnosis, my doctor put me on Insulin. With diabetes comes very dry skin, especially of the legs. The itch became so intense that I scratched my right leg so badly that I caused a sore that was so bad that not only did I end up in the hospital, but a visiting nurse from Merrimack Valley came to my home every day for five days straight to change the bandage. Diabetics are well known for losing their legs. My grandmother lost a leg, my great aunt lost two and my mother lost one.

The VA sent me a bottle of ammonium lactate which I applied every morning and night to stop the itch. I did this for years. Then, one Sunday when I was at Mass, my right leg began to itch and I began to scratch. I knew that to keep from getting another sore on my lower leg, I was going to have to go home, two miles away. It was about 7:50 a.m. with Mass beginning sharply at 8:00 a.m. I then prayed to St Jacinta Marto of Fatima to please help me so I wouldn't miss Mass and receiving the Eucharist. Immediately, the itch left my leg and I stopped scratching. As the days and weeks passed, I started using the cream less and less. This happened around 2016, with my use of ammonium lactate reducing to where it now has been at least a year since I needed to apply the cream.

Though there are other miracles I could write about, I will tell of only one more.

On Friday, June 11, 1999, I was living on South Broadway in Lawrence, MA. Something happened which caused me to suffer a great deal. The very next morning, I drove to St. Augustine's Church in Andover. When I went forward to receive the Eucharist, I put out my two hands and the priest placed the Host in my left hand. As I looked down at the Host before consuming it, it began to bleed. The only thing I could do was to place the Host in my mouth and consume it. By the time, the Host was in my mouth and before I swallowed it, the Host became soggy. Although I am now 76 years old, this unique experience has only happened once.

I could write of another miracle, but if you still don't accept the existence of a Supreme Being, then I'm not going to waste my time.

J. Douglas Barry

One more small miracle?

Many years ago, back in the 80's, I was in a Lawrence hospital. I don't recall why. It was, however, necessary for me to have my blood drawn.

Early in the morning, a young man came to draw my blood. When he stuck my arm, I never felt the needle go in. In the afternoon, the same young man came back to draw blood again. When he stuck me this time, I jumped from the pain. He remarked, "Wow. You didn't even move this morning." I then remarked, "That's because I said a small prayer."

There was total silence after that and I never saw him again. I really believe that the young man was also an atheist. God used me to probably save the man's soul.

There is an important message here about God's love for mankind. If I, a mortal man, can stop pain by a simple prayer, is it even more possible for the Son of God to prevent those nails in His hands and feet from causing any pain? This fact shows how much Jesus loves us in suffering for mankind and thereby atoning for our sins before God His Eternal Father and opening the gates of Heaven. It also shows you how much God loves you by bringing a person such as I together with your brother in order to give you a chance to believe in the existence of the Supreme Being and our Creator.

Remember, Marc, there is no end to Eternity.

ADDENDUM

08-10-20

I recently wrote an eight-page letter to a young atheist man. He wanted me to tell him about some of the miracles that have occurred in my life, and more than one. Since that letter, I recalled another miracle that happened on a mountain in New Hampshire.

Back in the early nineties, when I was working for the Internal Revenue Service (IRS), I was involved with the Cambodian children in Lawrence, MA. I wanted to take twenty children on both a mountain trip and a swim in the nearby lake, only I did not have enough money to do so. I said a small prayer and the very next day, I won $500.00 on a Lottery scratch ticket. I asked a lady at the IRS if she would like to help by taking five children in her car while I took fifteen in a rented van.

Then, on Saturday, we gathered up the twenty children and off we went to Bruce Mountain way up in New Hampshire. When we began to climb, it was already past noon as I remember. My good friend, Sister Helen O'Leary of the Sisters of Charity and the founder of the Saint Elizabeth Ann Seton Asian Center in Lawrence, MA. was praying to the Good Lord to keep me and the children safe. Why, she even told me her prayer when we got back. She prayed "Dear Lord, please wrap your arms around Doug and the children and keep them safe."

We had climbed halfway up and the hour was getting late, almost 3 PM. I decided that if we continued to climb, it would be dark before we got to the top, so against the wishes of the children, I decided to turn around and go back down the mountain and head off to the lake to go swimming.

As we began our trip down, I saw a man, probably in good shape by his build, wearing a plaid shirt, like a Lumber Jack's. He was walking up the mountain and to the left of us. Nobody said "hi", nor did he. I recall now that as he passed, he made no eye contact with anyone. As he passed me, the last one in our group, I slowly turned around just to see him, only there was no one there. Being so surprised, I asked the kids "What happened to the man who just passed us?", and every child plus the other adult with us said there was no man. I asked them what did they mean, he just walked by us. Again, they said that no one had passed.

When we got back, I told Sister Helen about this and she asked me what time this had occurred. When I told her the approximate time, she remarked that it was then that she had said the prayer mentioned above.

J. Douglas Barry

www.ingramcontent.com/pod-product-compliance
Lightning Source LLC
Chambersburg PA
CBHW082040080526
44578CB00009B/792